Sunrise to Sunset
(and all that lies between)

A Collection of Poetry
by
H. E. McIntyre

American Literary Press
Five Star Special Edition

Baltimore, Maryland

Sunrise to Sunset

Copyright © 2008 Howard E. McIntyre

All rights reserved under International and Pan-American copyright conventions. No part of this book may be reproduced, stored in a retrieval system, or transmitted in any form, electronic, mechanical, or other means, now known or hereafter invented, without written permission of the publisher. Address all inquiries to the publisher.

Library of Congress
Cataloging-in-Publication Data
ISBN-13: 978-1-934696-08-8

Library of Congress Card Catalog Number:
2008901876

Photography by H.E. McIntyre
Front cover: 'Birth of a New Day'
    (Virginia Beach on author's sixty-ninth birthday, November 2, 2006)
Back cover: Top - 'Sunset over Baltimore'
    (shot across the bay from Rock Hall, Maryland)
        Bottom - 'Sunset on Fence and Field'
    (farm field in Cecil County, Maryland)

Author photo by John Foehrkolb
    (Author at ENNWR, Rock Hall, Maryland)

Published by

American Literary Press
Five Star Special Edition

8019 Belair Road, Suite 10
Baltimore, Maryland 21236

Manufactured in the United States

Table of Contents

Preface .... vii-viii

Section I Starting The Journey: Who and What We Are

Tell Me Grandpa 1

Small Grand World 3

First Breast 6

Mellon Man 7

Pickled Onions 8

Frat Party 9

A Golden Mound Of Memories 11

Brief Silent Moments 12

When We Were Kids 13

Come Not Too Soon Sweet Spring 14

Section II Scotland: Home to My Forebearers

My Soul Was Once In Scotland 15

The Revenge of Glencoe 17

Scotsmen's Souls 18

He Cuts and Carries Bog Peat 19

Section III Nature: To Be Protected, Respected and Enjoyed

Sunrise, Clouds and Sea 20

Metamorphosis 21

The Nocturnal Symphony 22

Fawn Reflected 24

One Glorious Day 25

The River 27

Red Runs The River 28

An Old Man and His Bateau 29

The Seafood Store 30

Another Eastern Shore Cove 32

Shape Shifting 34

Song to a Bird 35

Elysian Field Has Gone to Sea 36

Unlearned Lessons 37

Section IV The Human Condition: Man's Inhumanity to Man

When Had Santa Become a Myth? 39

Man Should Not Make Bombs! 40

What Have The Children Done? 41

Her Eyes 42

White Flags and Dear Sweet Flowers 44

When Did Birds Stop Being Our Friends? 45

When Man Regains His Soul 46

The Invisible Man 47

Right The Wrong 49

Section V Spirituality: Man's Never Ending Search For Meaning

The Light 50

And All That Was, Was 51

I Saw Within The Mountain 53

The Voyeur 54

The Voice 56

Who Knows Where 57

Man's Merciful God 58

The Time Has Come 60

The Soul 61

Over Yonder 62

Section VI Emotions and Feelings: Love and Relationships

Abstract Art 63

Sometimes I Cry 64

A Child, A Flower, A Poignant Moment 65

I, The Man 66

Life Without You 67

They Live In Memories 68

Hands 69

By The Roadside Selling Her Wares 70

Christina 71

He Heard The Bells 73

She Blushes 74

Section VII   For Fun:
Into Every Life There Should Be Injected A Little Fun

Just About Everything 75

A Little Bit of This And 76

Tithing The Cat 77

Roaches Rule 79

Do Goldfish Have a Soul? 81

Crickets, Black Roosters and Crows 82

Ants Work, Cats Play 83

Hash House Harriers 83

The Leaf 84

Preface

This volume of poetry contains poems selected from over four hundred of my poems. I had thought to publish my poems in chronological order as they were written by date and year. However, after reviewing the idea with my publisher, I thought it best to organize the poems in some meaningful order (at least to me) and showcase my favorites. This distillation of my work draws from the time I started writing poetry in 2004 to present. (A book of poetry, *Turtles Never Cheat, Lie or Steal*, for young readers has been completed and scheduled for publication later in 2008.)

Sometime during the dreary winter month of January 2004, Lynne, my wife, and I, seeking something mind-stimulating to do, registered for courses in the Life Long Learning Program presented at Washington College in Chestertown, Maryland. One of the courses was The Pleasures of Poetry conducted by Mr. David Hilton. The classes were just over one hour in length, six sessions reduced to five due to a snowstorm cancellation of night one. Mr. Hilton provided examples of many poem forms supported by excellent samples of a variety of poets' works. The course triggered thoughts hidden deep in my mind and soul. It's frightening what happened as a result of this experience. After the first night I began to write and write and write—the floodgates were opened. Thank you, David (posthumously).

I have tried to include poems that reflect a little of my growing up—the times, people and places. The environment and nature are of great interest to me as you will see in poems on these topics. I am blessed to live in an area where I experience first hand every day the beauty and wonder of nature. My hobbies of photography, kayaking, birding and fishing, I think, have honed my eye to see much of what the casual observer sees—but "does not see." I, as you surely will see, am also very concerned about man's stewardship of our most-valued treasures—our children and Mother Earth.

Like most poets I ponder our very existence, from whence we came, how should we live and where we go from here. I question man's actions, inactions and motivation in his relationship with others and his surroundings. My concept of God, the soul and life in general is voiced from both my own beliefs and those of scholars, philosophers and bards of the past.

I have also enjoyed experimenting with a variety of forms of poetry: rhyming poems, free verse, Ertheree, Sestina, "Shape" poems, sonnet and haiku.

I would like to thank my wife Lynne, my family and friends and others with whom I have shared my poetry for their interest and support. I would like to specifically thank Susan Argo, Kent County Poet in Residence, for her valued comments and support and allowing me to work with her and the Bainbridge Elementary School children. I treasure the experience of sharing my poetry at several venues in the Chestertown area: Play It Again Sam, The Prince Theater, Andy's and the Mainstay in Rock Hall. Leslie and Vincent Raimond of the Kent County Arts Council have been especially supportive of both my poetry and photography. Finally, thanks to Ann Hennessy (*Becoming Ann: A Baltimore Childhood*, a memoire published by American Literary Press) and our writing group for their comments and support and Ann for directing me to American Literary Press.

I am indebted to Ann Hennessy, Donna Wessel (American Literary Press) and my brother Bill for their help in reading and editing my many drafts of this book. It takes a great deal of courage to face my work in its raw state—my spelling, punctuation and misuse of certain words. Thank you all from the depths of my creative heart.

I hope that I am successful in hitting a nerve with you the reader. And that you are both challenged and entertained. Thank you for joining me on my journey.

H.E.McI

This collection of my poetry is divided into seven sections reflecting on certain aspects of my life and, I suspect, the lives of my readers. The first section deals with my formative years and those things in life that shape, encourage and gradually erode one's body and mind. The second section bespeaks of my Scottish heritage, and the third my interest and passion for nature and my concern for man's mismanagement of Mother Earth. This leads directly into the fourth section, which deals with the human condition and man's inhumanity to man.

The role of a supreme being, spirituality and the search for a purpose in life seemed to be a necessary follow-up to the nature of man. At this juncture I felt a need to interject some *amore*—poems on feelings and relationships—and tail off with some lighter poetry.

I hope that your read is as much fun for you as it was for me over the past four years in writing and editing these poems.

Thank you for joining me on this journey.

Section I. Starting The Journey: Who And What We Are

Tell Me Grandpa

Clink, clink
The juice glass
Tapped the cereal bowl
As I carried his breakfast tray.
"Grandpa, tell me of the sea and ships."
He stared through gray-glazed eyes.

"Tell me of your life in Scotland
And when you were just my age.
Tell me how you earned your passage
When you were but a boy.
How was the ocean and its crossing,
The perils that you endured?
Tell me, Grandpa, tell me just once more."
Milk dripped from his unshaven chin.

"Grandpa, where did you first land
And how did you get here?
You worked so hard to make a life
And then you took Grandma to be your wife."
He slowly reached to get his pipe.

"Tell me how you pitched and hit
That homer when you played baseball.
Were the tattoos that you wear
From when you sailed the seas?
Will I be able to drink beer like you
When I'm a grown up man?"
*He packed tobacco into his pipe
With a gnarled, bony finger.*

"When you broke your nose that time
Riding on a bare-back horse,
Did it hurt as much as when you broke your leg
 Climbing up a mountain side
 Or falling from that tree?
When the Germans shot at you
Did you shoot some dead?"
*He jiggled a tiny cardboard box
And raked a match along its side.*

"Grandpa, are we going hiking
Deep into Bay-view woods?
Can we fish the old mill pond
Or roller skate the new state road?
Will you carry me piggy-back
To see the tigers in the zoo?"
*The flame of the match glowed red
on his snow-white cheeks,
and shadowed his wrinkled brow
and the deep cleft in his chin.*

"Grandpa did they have schools
When you were but a boy?
Papa says that you didn't go to school—
How then did you get so smart?
You know just about everything,
The stars that light the night,
The flowers, trees and birds.
You know their names and what they do."
He puffed and stared through glassine eyes.
Muted were his lips.

"Grandpa, where is Grandma now
And your mom and dad?
Do you wish that they were here
Or you were there with them?
I hope you never leave—
I would miss you so ..."
His eyes moistened
As he turned his head away.
Later that day—
I found him ...

Small Grand World

In my youth my world was bound
By a back lot, a fence and
Row houses eight blocks around
My house was in the center of one row
Beyond two blocks in either way—
I was forbid to go
The back barren lot beyond my alley
Was all my imagination allowed it to be.

The vast vacant lot was shaped like an 'L'
I knew every cranny and nook of it well
The hill at back topped by a very high fence
It was a firm boundary but gave recompense
For climbing it opened the door
To many more places a young child's mind could explore.

Bound by the fence was a hall and Finlander's home
A wonderful interesting place to roam
The caretakers were 'Fins,'—caring and kind
Allowed us their entry—as long as we'd mind
They told us stories of their northern cold land
Of wonderful places so beautiful and grand.

During the winter the snow-covered hill
Was a glacier-filled mountain to me
I climbed to the top—testing my will
Oh, what wonderland there I could see
Pulling packed round drifts of snow
Rollicking and rolling down the hill I'd go.

In summer the vacant lot of grass and stone
Was a calm, great place too—to be all alone
Or ball fields, bowling lawn, a place of jousting
It offered a space for children's rough housing
Many memorable games did we have there
Seeds planted in a young child's mind—so fresh—so rare.

The baseball field with ever-changing boundaries
Tried but lost the wars with youth's boundless energies
A red brick, a broken building block and a board
Were the bases we rounded as the runs we scored
The bat had been broken so many times
It gave pinches and splinters and hurts of all kinds
The tar-taped ball the pitcher threw
Was the only baseball that we kids knew.

In the far distance of the vast vacant 'L'
Stood the remains of a building that fell
What a great fort the foundation could be
We'd fight with each other or an imagined enemy
It was the sight of many heroic battles
(Little brother's hurt—runs home and tattles.)

Lest one thinks the back lot a mere pleasure
It worked us kids hard—taking our measure
Laying out fields was sometimes hard
As was retrieving a foul ball from a neighbor's yard
And especially bad was the window we'd break
We'd flip to see who would fix it—and apology make.

The back lot was also the place of communal gatherings
Birthday parties, seasonal celebrations and gossip blatherings
But grandest by far were my dad's picture shows
Given for gathered neighbors—sitting in rows
Rented pictures projected on a white bed sheet
Daring divers from Acapulco the program'd complete.

Every neighbor and neighborhood kid
would sit on the edge of his chair
To watch suspended divers twisting,
Turning and tumbling in air
But one of our greatest rewards—a very strange thing
Was to run the reel in reverse—a sight to behold
As up from the water the divers would spring
Return to the top of the cliff and faulty foothold.

At the age of seven my parents relented
Removing those boundaries I sometimes resented
Beyond the lot, the hill and the fence
To places beyond a child's comprehence
And now that I look back on it so
My parents knew when to trust and let go.
          3/20/04

First Breast

While riding a trolley
in East Baltimore
down the one lone block
where black people lived—
descendants of servants
of clipper ship captains
and wealthy merchants
who lived up the hill—
I remember it still.

Down in Canton
on that lone black block
sat a young black woman
on a white marble stoop
with her breast— bronzed and bare—
and a blanketed baby
who suckled it there
I could not react
I sat there aghast
the view from the trolley
went by so fast
2/15/04

Melon Man

"Water melons,
water melons—
fresh melons,"
melon man cried

The women
neighborhood women
his melons
they'd buy

Melon cart
swayed back horse
back alley 'A-rab'—
"melons for sale"

Thunked melons
green melons
sweet melons
they put in a pail

Beautiful carriage
proud white stallion glides
neighborhood kids
sneaked— magnificent rides

"Water melons.
fresh melons..."
melon man
cried

Hoof beats
echoe's that swell
manure droppings
pungent sweet smell

Creaking wagon
wooden sides stress
creak ... creak ... creak
with every sway

Bang twang—bang twang
the swinging scale
to weigh melons
hung from the rail

Whinnying echoes
the wagon rolled on
water melons—no melons
melon man ...
has gone!
                        2/17/04

Pickled Onions

Yellow—
Sour, sweet
Pickled onions
Lexington Market on shopping day.

Trolley cars
And belching buses
Taxi cabs with blaring horns
Shopping bags
Large, brown
Shopping bags.

Pungent fishy smells
Sounds of shoveled ice
Wet, slippery floors
Hawkers crying,
"Comeandbuymywares."

Panzer's pickles
Wooden salt brine barrels
Pig's feet in large glass jars.
Traffic music and echoing voices
Smoke rings from men's
Big
Fat
Cigars.

Foot long 'dogs'
And butcher's stalls
Mustached men
In pictures
Hanging on
Darkened
Dingy
Walls.

Ladies waddling
With heavy loads
Kids lagging behind
Lugging bags
Large—
Brown—
Shopping bags.
A week of groceries
To haul back home
Over miles
And miles
Of roads.

Saturday
The shopping day
Almost as sacred as Sunday
We kids could have
Cotton candy
Or taffy treats—
Me?
I'd have—
pickled onions.
    6/17/07

Frat Party

"How do you feel?"
A voice asked from out of the fog.
I thought, "hum, where the hell am I?"
Retracing my steps I slowly remembered
Clothes spread from bed to door
Aspirin bottle and ten spilled pills
Did I drive home or did I walk?

Stumbled, was my guess
Stairs, lots of stairs
Why hadn't I taken the elevator
Maybe I had, I don't know
Loud music, lots of talking, singing, shouting,
Laughter and some tears—
Woosh! someone had just tapped another keg.

Beer, lots of beer and a couple of shots
A drag on some weed, I think that was all
The food was great for eating—
Occasional organic art or flying missiles
A collage of ketchup, mustard,
Lettuce, tomatoes and olives—
And eggs adorned the kitchen floor.

Young men and women were coupled
Some sharing a couch, a chair—the floor.
How is it that off-key singing
And forgotten words seem
To sound so good?
I don't think I made that crash
But the broken mirror stood there before me
My face in a thousand shards
And hers webbed there beside me.

Why her? Was she in my Spanish class
Or was it Biology—no, no, Philosophy.
Yes, yes, oh, she was the smart one
She could quote Socrates
And poetry of the Bard.
She smelled of sweet spring flowers
Her mouth a rose-red orb
Her skin a soft light tan
A smile lined with white pearl teeth—
A goddess in a satin sheath.

I thought frat brothers were
Faithful, kind and true
What part of our oath had he broken
The way he looked at her—
The way he spoke?
He clearly spoke a language
They both had understood
And as they walked through
The bedroom door

I saw his eyes and hers
A mixture of pity, shame and sorrow
Was rage justified—
I hardly knew the girl.

In the distance
My roommate asked again,
"How do you feel?"
Looking down at my bandaged hand
I said,
       "I really feel like shit!"
              9/18/09

A Golden Mound of Memories

The leaves swirled tornado round
The leaves I raked, the children found
They rolled, tossed and frolicked there
Kids at play without a care.

The laughs the screams did my heart good
A welcome sound to the neighborhood
They'd run and dive into the leaves
Tuck them in their pants and sleeves.

They'd ride my barrow like kings and queens
Upon the leaves through tree-bare scenes
Into the woods where I'd haul the leaves
Then hide away like common thieves.

Each would sneak behind a tree
Then jump out and 'boo' at me
I'd grab my chest and fall away
They'd jump and laugh in joyful play.

We'd made these trips for years it seems
I shared their play, their high-pitched screams
Through the years we'd alter themes
I raked the leaves of childhood dreams.

I gathered the leaves again today
The children have grown and moved away
I gazed into the pile of leaves—
A golden mound of memories ...
                              11/11/06

Brief Silent Moments
for John, his sister Marilyn, and my mom

Standing by a woods,
the sun slowly retreating,
rays barely peaking
above the skeletal trees—
the "who, who-who"
of a great horned owl
breaks the silence. Cool
is the breeze upon the air.

A clink of glasses
as two friends salute,
a wee amber dram,
warm and soothing. Again
the night owl hoots—
a lonely, haunting sound—
each friend lost in thought.

A mother stands before the one,
thoughts of a long-lost sister
prevails upon the other. Each man
in silence visits with his apparition.
Both share a lifetime
in those brief silent moments.

Their reverie again is broken
as the owl speaks to the night.
Each raises the remnant
of his single malt,
savors the last of the toast
in a knowing shared silence ...
                        12/30/06

When We Were Kids

The sky looked much higher then
The snow much deeper in the glen
Those simple things within our ken—
When we were kids.

Our thoughts were innocent, clear and pure
We were immortal—
not knowing what life had in store
... no consequence *then* of a slamming door—
When we were kids.

A snowball fight was purely fun
It was meant to harm no one
We would frolic, roll and run—
When we were kids.

Our thoughts of life and worldly things
Were the joys of living and surviving bee stings
Of the musical sounds when a mockingbird sings
When we were kids.

What ever happened to those innocent days
Each morning starting with a new-found craze
When the simplest of things could still amaze
When we were kids.

Does growing older require a rent
A toll for the time of innocence spent
For our later sins we now repent
Far removed from when we were kids.

Does growing old and wiser cost
The innocence and purity that we have lost
Images fading in window-breath frost
When we were kids?

The mind is dulled of memories
Of special times and swings in trees
The naive talks of birds and bees
When we were kids.

When sitting silent in a rocking chair
Our fragile frame and smiling stare
In a pleasant place without compare
Where we were kids.

And those whom we have left behind
Have no entry into our mind
They fear false prisons where we're confined
Instead of those sweet times—
When we were kids!
                    10/28/05

Come Not Too Soon Sweet Spring

Come not too soon sweet spring
And crocus raise your head
Buds and blooms awake mid-season
And die of frost for no good reason.

As birds fly north in chase of spring
Winter winds chill flapping wings
The heart and soul that yearns for spring
The season spurns—a tragic thing.

Let winter's blasts retreat at last
And *gently* enter spring
A mix of color, sound and word
An artist's pallet, a poet's pen—
          the singing of a bird.

The subtle green of trees and grass
The smell of heather—lovely highland lass
Such sweet perfume as blossoms bloom
Free at last from winter's gloom.

And tho the spring will pass too soon
I'll savor every measure, every verse, every tune
Each spring a brand new treasure—then again it's June
And summer—prelude to the fall—
Then winter—harshest of them all—
The season of the loon.

Come not too soon sweet, sweet spring
For then you'll quickly fade away
And years will pass as quickly as a day
And *all too soon* the last church chimes shall ring.
                                      3/18/07

Section II. Scotland: Home to My Forebearers

My Soul Was Once In Scotland

A soul is something borrowed
Not entirely of one's self
The universal soul
Is marvelously undefined
Some eternal cosmic force
That passes through all things.

I've sensed a soul in all creatures
Every living thing
Birds and trees and cats and dogs

Beasts of every kind
Crickets have a special soul
They've shared with all humanity
From before man's measured time.

The mountains, wind and rain
Have within a mixing of the souls
Souls once troubled, needing mending
Rest as granite stone—
Sometimes there for many ages
Then nature does its grandest work
Through sun and ice and wind and rain
Breaks down the rigid stone
Releasing fresh-cleansed souls
To travel on their way.

Souls do not impose on those they are within
They lay in silence waiting
Encouraged by the ether soul
That flows within us all
And as one's soul matures it may—
Just may, receive a greater call.

My soul was once in Scotland
This I surely know
As I once trod Culloden Field
Ancestors' souls sang out to me
I did not feel the pain of death
Nor that of those who had fallen there
I felt a sense of unity
In their collective prayer.

2/27/06

The Revenge of Glencoe

Out of the crags of that moonlit moor
Came the cries of a clan lost to war
Of two clans that clashed for power and might
And in Glencoe—shed blood—that heinous night
When a Laird of the land his blood oath was broke
Accepting protection of his enemy host—he lied as he spoke!

Late at night the deceitful betrayer
Cautiously crept out of his layer
To clansmen a signal he gave from on high
Every Macdonald to the last should die!
And that became clan Campbell's cry
Every Macdonald to the last shall die—shall die!

And in their sleep those of the Macdonald clan
Were put to the sword every woman, child and man
Their ghosts haunt every valley and hill
The haunting voices of *those* the Campbells did kill
Having no kinsmen left to take up revenge
Their own sorrowful souls *they had* to avenge.

And down through the ages the stories unfold
Of strange deaths of Campbells both young and old
How chieftains in fright have gone insane
Out in Glencoe in horrible pain
And babies dying in mothers' wombs
Hearing the cries from Macdonalds' untended tombs.

And to this day Scotts fear to tread
On that hallowed ground of the long-lost dead
Especially there on a moonless night
Where the souls of Macdonalds are given to flight
In eerie song from the hills and the valley arise
We're nae ta rest 'til every Campbell—
      woman, child and man dies!
         3/29/04

Scotsmen's Souls

At dawn the fields
cast a dull, dark purple hue
from lack of the morning sun.

But as that flaming orb arises
the fields burst forth in brilliant glow—
the thistle comes alive.

Bees harvesting nectar
compete with butterflies. Goldfinch
have not yet arrived
to steal the thistle down.

Bull thistles love mountain meadows
by wandering streams and
great blue cloud-filled skies.

Their sharp spike thorn
can tear rawhide. White seed parachutes—
soft down for nests provide.

Thistles stand Scottish proud—
strong, rugged and hearty. Like lads
sent off to fight in wars.
Wars for other's wealth and power.
But thistle strong Scottish lads
fought for homeland, love and honor.

They say that thistles grow
in fields where Scotts have bled.
In far off lands—

where Scotsmen's lives were shed.
Each grand purple thistle
a Scottish soul—
        rugged; hearty ... tender.

11/14/06

He Cuts and Carries Bog Peat

He emerged out of the mist of a low-slung fog
Peat o'er his shoulder cut from primordial bog
Broad of shoulder and 'V'-ed to his waist
He plodded along in no great haste

He'd trod this trail ninety years or more
As had his father and *his* father before
The peat from the bog to heat his home
From the chill of north winds and the pending gloam

Aye, twas a hard life but he lived it well
There on the land where his forefathers fell
Defending a land where no man should live
Their lives for honor they would again give

He and his wife raised twelve children there
A life of joy and toil they shared
Thirteen cairns stand at the foot of a hill
A testament to his love and strong Scot's will

He sits each evening 'neath that gnarled tree
Mining his soul—his memory
Of the lives they had shared
The loved ones who'd cared

A tear erodes the grime on his cheek
His voice cracks as he tries to speak
"To you, my bonnie sweet wife
Thank you for sharing my wonderful life—

"And to you, my children, who gave me such joy
A mixture of courage, strength and love—
       a wondrous alloy

I cut and carried the peat today
To the home and hearth where you once played
"I don't know how many more days I can carry the load
Up from the bog on that rutted road

But in the warmth of that fire I feel each of you there
And I know in my heart you are with me and care
If you can but wait a little while more
I have to finish but one last chore
A cairn for myself right next to thee
And then forever—together we'll be!" 3/31/05

Section III. Nature: To be Respected, Protected and Enjoyed

Sunrise, Clouds and Sea

Sunrise seems so long to come
reluctant star, the rising sun
the clouds in layers await
to greet the sun's warm rays
when they both meet. The
dull gray clouds of early dawn
seem to stretch in sleepy yawn.

The first light soft and mute
gulls cry out a loud salute
pink now the clouds and sky
each new day I wonder why
I've never seen the sky the same—
a clouded mood—a brilliant flame.

The sea a coral-red, blue and gold
a story painted and retold
in days and years of old
earth's history on sea and sky is told.
Now so bright it hurts the eye
rays once brilliant fade and die.

The dawn has come and gone again
the sea lies calm—a blue-black plain.
Upon the air a hint of rain
no matter what I shall remain
to smell the air and taste the sea
and savor all its memory.
                              11/16/06

Metamorphosis

The flowers are alive with their second bloom
They blossom, flit and fly away.
Red Admirals, orange sulphurs and swallowtail
In colorful coats they all regale.

The butterflies have come to feed and breed
The pollen they spread gives rise to seed
Of plants that support butterflies, birds and bees
And flowers with aroma guaranteed to please.

Attracted to colors orange, yellow and red
Some prefer purple and blues instead
They crisscross the fields sampling each flower
They do this each morning 'til the noontime hour.

Butterflies thrive on the heat of the day
Where they go at night I truly can't say
But the beauty they give each day to me
Is a wonder of nature I am privileged to see.

One brief season and they fly on
Laying their eggs and then they are gone
Soon jiggling and squiggling as scars on the leaf
Betray the critters that crawl beneath.

Caterpillars emerge from thousands of eggs
A curious worm with horns, false eyes and legs
They munch on the flowers and green leaf plants
And fatten themselves as the cold days advance.

Then wrap up in leaves or spin a cocoon
Knowing that winter will be here too soon
During the cold of long nights and short days
The caterpillar changes in many strange ways.

In the heat of the summer and late spring heat
A new form emerges—what a wonderful treat
A beautiful blossom stretching its wings
One of nature's most glorious things.

The cycle continues as the wheel of time
Rolls out the mystery—of reason and rhyme
One of life's wonders revealed to man
Is it by chance or some divine plan?
7/27/07

The Nocturnal Symphony

The sun has set and
    in the cool of the evening
    the chorus begins.

Like howling wolves
    it seems always
    to start with one.

One lone peep
    answered by two
    soon a choir of peeps
    drowns the night air.

A burping cow
    in a bucket croaks
    answered by a splashing friend—
    lover, friend or foe?

A second chorus
    in a southern voice
    runs a thumb
    'cross a metal comb.

Joined by cricket-like notes
    a rasping snore
    and a nasal alarm—
    The night is alive.

A whip-o-will sounds his approval
    with that of a night-jar—
    squeals of bats, and a hooting owl.

Out of the darkness
    a high shrill scream
    the barn owl has silenced the night.

For hour-long seconds
    the night is still
    then as if on cue—one peep
    and the nocturnal chorus
    resumes.

                        3/6/06

Fawn Reflected

As I awakened by that pool
The morning air, a pleasant cool
Smoke in tendril spires arise
Looking through sleepy—
               half-closed eyes
Reflections of a fawn appear
The young girl-child of a white-tail deer

As if by the twitching of her ear
Ringlets roll in water once clear
'Pond fawn' is ever flowing—
standing deer not knowing
Her image shimmers gently there
Does she know—does she care

Gently down her head she dips
Lapping water tongue and lips
Reflected fawn's spots run and race
Planets revolve in outer space
Standing fawn stealthily stretches
Floating fawn waning moon's—
                     reflection catches
Moon and planets swirling there
Standing fawn still unaware

Fawn's head snaps quickly to attention
Showing fear and apprehension
Her ears twist and turn around
Seeing, sensing silent sound
Relief appears in simple form
That from which the fawn was born
Mother deer gently licks her velvet coat
As only nature's caring mothers mote
Soft elongated lipid eyes
Reflecting pools in other guise
Fawn's pure image standing there
In her mother's fond and loving stare. 5/1/04

One Glorious Day

Fog on white wet wings descends
obscures the lake from its both ends
The rising sun burns off the fog
disclosing there a berry bog
A fawn laps cool water there
sees her reflection—becomes aware
A strange brown beast before her lies
two long ears and slanting eyes
Afraid that she's a predator's prey
lightly she leaps and bounds away.

A pebble dislodged, crashed into the pond
creating circles hither and yond
On the leaf of a lily pad and its bright bloom
a big green frog sits there to groom
He vainly looks at his reflection
not seeing the waves in his direction
He's bounced from the leaf into the drink
that he could swim, surely, one would think
He foundered and struggled, sunk to the mud
and there was a grasshopper chewing his cud.

What's a grasshopper doing here
the frog sarcastically asked of him
Now isn't your question queer
oh talking frog who can not swim
Help me, help me! I'm drowning cried the frog
the grasshopper dragged him out of the berry bog
And on the bank as they both preened
a great blue heron from a tree branch leaned
Swooping down was no big deal
in two gulp, gulps she had a meal.

The great blue heron flew back on nest
squawking and flapping with the rest
A sea of snakes in the tops of the trees
swaying their necks in a fresh cool breeze
She regurgitated the 'hopper' and frog
for nestlings—a warm, fermented grog
The rookery becomes quiet, all fast asleep
no time for the young to count their sheep
A clap of thunder booms in the air
catching the rookery unaware.

Lightning flashing and thunder crashing
branches gnashing—nestlings thrashing
One nest topples, drops to the ground
and there by chance the nestlings are found
By a large green grotesque lizard
who swallowed them down to his blood-red gizzard
He lumbered on limply along his way
expelling dung drops with every sway
Dung beetles soon arrived at the feast
not bothered by the smell were they in the least
They soon rendered the huge piles down
nutrients to nourish the fertile ground
Seeds left there from a previous meal
with the heat from the sun began to reveal
A new growth of green from the forest floor
replenishing food to Mother Nature's store.

Honey bees and humming birds
communicating with their bee-bird words
Nectar is drunk and pollen spread
creating the new while using the dead
Green leafed plants bask in the sun
storing its energy till day is done
As evening nears the fawn appears
twisting and turning its ears

It nibbles at grass—its energy source
merging full grown in time's due course
And such is the cycle of life
the new is created through trials, tribulation and strife.

The old die off—some young die too
all added to Mother Nature's stew
Green plants processing the rays of the sun
life's energy source since time begun
All living things are born, procreate and die
those that crawl, walk, slither and fly

Those with roots or live on air
and those who kneel in solemn prayer
All are players in nature's grand play
and will know its meaning one glorious day.
       3-5/19/06

The River

His bateau was a hollow log
A tree branch served as tiller and oar
He speared fish with a sapling stick
Sharpened with his knife of stone.

The river, unforgiving
Took his life one day
His family knew not
Where he had gone to stay
He was just gone
To be seen no more.

His son fished the same bateau
Steered it with the same tree branch
Sharpened spears with broken stone
Following in his father's footsteps
The river is a patient beast.
       7/16/06

Red Runs the River

The river
a nameless swollen stream
ran through the village
runoff from a mountain lake
and monsoon rains
the village
ten thatched huts
on either side
winter-summer homes
the cattle
scrawny scrub-fed
mostly ribs and bones
the herdsman
also ribs and bones
one small bone in his nose
and in one ear
the fish
I think pirana
is their name
each year the cattle cross
by river ford
the nameless swollen stream
one cow
near death crosses
below the herd
downstream
red
runs the river
flesh, flow and fish
meet as one
a sacrifice
to the river gods
the herd crosses safely

glassy-eyed
the herdsman
holds his pipe
in his two-fingered hand
he too
had appeased the river gods.
                    11/12/06 (1:00 a.m.)

An Old Man and His Bateau

The sea oats hid all but the brim
of his weathered straw hat. They
hushed the knock of his oar
as it rapped the wooden side
of his skiff. The crunching sound
of reeds preceded the bow of the boat—
a square-bow bateau—favored
by men of the South as platforms
for fishing and crabbing.

Some hunted these boats for swan,
duck and geese; but he,
at just over one hundred, had passed
through that stage in his life. He
now poled the pram as a water hiker,
through paths in the marshes
and salt-flat bays. He'd just sit,
watch and listen to the sound
of the rushes, the birds and the wind.
Occasionally he'd whistle
a familiar bird tune in conversational reply.

He'd seen the sun rise and set many times.
He never tired of the moon, the water,
his marshland home. He wanted his ashes
spread on an outgoing tide. And
his wooden bateau set free.   11/24/06

The Seafood Store

The smell of fish
was raw and rank
five kittens scurried
from stall to stall
lapping oyster liquor
and gnawing meat
from fresh fish bones.

One black man
shucked oysters all the day
while another skinned
and fileted fish never scaling
or gutting them—
staking the larger ones.

The glass-front cases
displayed oysters, mussels
and clams a variety of whole,
fileted and staked fish,
turtle, scallops and squid.

The oiled wooden floors
were pathed in worn wood trails
sawdust here and there
soaked up blood and liquor
fish eyes peaked out
from ice-filled barrels.

The salesgirl spoke
in an island lilt her smiling face
sat upon a full round chest
her legs were ample support
for her hefty frame.

The door hinges squealed
from their labors as patrons
came and went
they sounded like
loose metal oar locks
as bateau went from shore
to fishing boats.

An almost tuned radio
blared from the shucking room
along with static and
occasional mumbling
between the two black men—
I think they are brothers.

I entered craving seafood
I left with more than I could eat
I'll freeze the scallops and oysters
and fry the fish today—
the clams and mussels
we'll eat before the fish.

The parking lot
was sand and shell
high tides and heavy rain
left pothole lakes and
strands of seaweed wreaths.

The wooden shack
they called a store
had never seen a coat of paint
the porch had once been screened
now more holes than screen
the crawl space was home
to fat feral cats.

A one-eyed dog lay comatose
on wood floor planks
the only sign of life
a half-hearted slap of his tail
one drumbeat on seasoned oak
bid farewell
as we drove away.
     11/13/06

Another Eastern Shore Cove

Coils of line lay lazily
   over an old rusted boat anchor
Equally decayed were an old patten-tong rig
   and an antique iron hauling cart

A half-standing crab shanty
   gave entrance to a broken-down pier
The squeaking of a broken weather vane
   on the farthest piling—

Blended with the squeals and cries of gulls
   as they dove and fought for morsels of food
They had neatly whitewashed
   each of the remaining rotting wooden timbers

The breeze and gentle lapping of waves
   sang in unison a lulling tune
Black and turkey vultures
   rode great merry-go-rounds in the sky

A red-tailed hawk and two immature eagles
   flew in and out of the ride
An old one-lunger could be herd coughing
   lunk-lunk-lunking up in the river's haze

Clunk-screech, clunk-screech
   the sound of an oarsman at work

Rowing an old Van Sant bateau
            out to a waterman's crabbing rig

Sixty crab pots adorned the roof and deck
            cabin walls coated in rust
The thirty-foot-long wood boat
            hadn't seen a coat of paint in years

A muted 'clang' . . . 'clang-clang'
            sounded from distant channel buoy
It's barnacled frame had welcomed
            mariners to the cove for over seventy years

As if on command two mute swan
            ran flapping to flight from the water

The wind through their wings
            and sway of their serpentine necks
      Gave chorus and movement to an aerial ballet
           silhouetted in the rising sun
Orange gold reflecting on rippling waters
            the last of the spring peepers were croaking

A young boy shouts in glee
            as his bobber is pulled from view
His cane pole bends
            under the weight of a ten-pound catfish

His dog lifts his sleepy head
            and slaps his wagging tail in approval on the pier
"Hey, mister, can you take this fish off the hook for me?"
            He beamed as he asked— how could I refuse?

I pinned back the pectoral spines
            and removed the hook from the dead-eyed 'cat'
I wiped the slime on my jeans—
            some things seem never to change.
                        3/19/05

Shape Shifting

The sun arose on desert sand
and as if by some grand command
shadows grew and sand scenes changed
rock and plants all rearranged.

Colors mute became alive
when west winds began to drive
spirits from the earth and sky
on what images could the mind rely?

Charging horses, buffalo
on and on the wild herds go
cries of children ride the wind
torment raged from deep within.

Shaman shadows on canyon walls
lone wild wolf to lost mate calls
gone to sleep the river bed
water on which wild weeds fed.

The cactus grew to giant size
only then to realize
gone was the grand lush view
colored meadows where flowers grew.

A shaman then appeared to me
look around at all you see
the flowing river the thundering herds—
all this said in foreign words—

Remember now the birds long gone
listen to the do-do's song
hear the lone wolf's cry
see the empty endless sky—

Taste the water no longer there
kneel and say a silent prayer
that he who made the land and earth
will forgive us all and give rebirth.

The shaman shape began to shift
a raven then began to drift
above the vast and vacant land
a shadow cast on shifting sand.
       12/04/06

Song to a Bird

Sorry I cannot whistle
  or play a soothing flute
  nor trill a high-pitched chorus
  my repertoire is short and sweet.
  I'll just sing for you—
    tweet, tweet-tweet.

I envy you, oh, one who flies
  among the clouds up in the skies
  your travels here and far away
  your hard work and aerobatic play
  your nest compact, soft and neat
  I sing for you—
    tweet, tweet-tweet.

Would that I could sing your song
  I'd sing it loud and all day long.
  I wish I had your steadfast care
  for your young within the nest you share.
  I long to have your life complete.
  I sing to you—
    tweet, tweet-tweet.

    And when you leave and fly away
        I'll think of you each new day
        I'll wonder where you have gone
        what songs you sang at early dawn
        and if again we should meet—
        I'll share once more— your sweet—
                      tweet-tweet.
                          11/16/06

Elysian Field Has Gone To Sea
Dedicated to those still suffering the effects of Katrina.

Elysian Field has gone to sea
Bodies set sail in tiny cement and wood-clad ships
The blues turn to brown and red with the rise of the tide
Rooftop survivors wave signs of distress
While looters wave guns and steal food and regress
Water, water everywhere
The town of New Orleans has drown!

The biegnet are soggy, the town is a mime
Silently swimming in a swirling storm
St. James Square is a public pool
For waders in over their head
The living, half-living— the dead
I'd give my bottle of bourbon for a drink of pure water instead
The town of New Orleans has drown!

The bell of a trumpet gleams up from the mud
A mongrel dog holds tightly to a floating bass drum
The silent music falls on dead ears
The saints are marching, but hear no cheers
The funeral dirge has been played by the winds
Followed by an entourage of flying glass, cement and tree limbs
The town of New Orleans has drown!

The City of Saints, its soul in distress,
Sodden—no more room for tears
Awash from the gulf, the river and Pontchartrain lake
The friendly water that washed its shores now sneers
Turned hostile by whirling winds and raging rain
Sorrow's the tune the jazz band plays over and over again
The town of New Orleans has drown!

Down on the levy or where the levy used to be
No banjos are playing, no music is making
Just the surging of water and misery
But in the memories of saints the souls will arise
To a glorious and better day
The saints *will* come marching in again
The crowds will cheer and the music will flow ...
        ... as the town of New Orleans survives!
                9/01/05

Unlearned Lessons

When last I heard the Raven sing
Soaring round on cold black wing
The mountain stood in regal pride
Grand redwood forests greened its side
And waterfalls roared while grinding rocks
Gray jays massed in giant flocks.

The mountain lion and grizzly bear
Roamed there doomed but unaware
As were their forest friends
And mountain vistas without ends
A land so beautiful without compare
One the greedy could not share.

They cut the trees and raped the land
Disregarding what God had planned
They killed the lion and the bear
They dammed the streams and fouled the air
They took and took, gave nothing back
The mountain then began to crack.

The mighty giant had had enough
It began to swell, steam and puff
Followed by a belching roar
Its tremors reached the ocean floor
Nature's fireworks filled the sky
To survive—the mountain would have to die.

Molten magma in lava flows
Woodland creatures fled in droves
Half of the mountain spread across the land
Beaches covered in gray-ash sand
The sun shown not for many days
And on the air a sad song plays.

In twenty years the land restores
Trees too young, so man ignores
But in the future some early morning
Greedy men heed not the warning
They cut, kill, rape and burn
When will mankind ever learn?
When will mankind *ever* learn!
                              8/21/04

Section IV. The Human Condition:
Man's Inhumanity to Man and Nature

When Had Santa Become A Myth?

He, white haired, stooped yet standing
    watched grandchildren play
    a pleasure—undemanding
    a solace, mixed with dismay.

The children frolicked, skipped and ran
    the greatest pleasure given man
    the innocense of our childhood days
    and in his mind he replays—

When as a child he too had played
    and by the shore sand castles made
    he'd fought the dragons and played with toys
    he reveled in a young child's joys.

When had Santa become a myth
    and Easter Bunny along with—
    heroes of his past
    why couldn't our childhood's last?

He looked again into their loving eyes
    and much to his surprise
    he saw a knowing glance—
    in each child—a new-found chance.
                      12/16/06

Man Should Not Make Bombs!
(Influenced by my reading of *The New Yorker*)
(Happy Birthday, Dee)

      I had taken to peeing in the kitty litter
      in the box abandoned by my squirrelly cat—
      selling the hardened sculptures
      at a gallery in So Ho. These
      and verses of scatologically correct poetry
      sold like hot cakes—
                    Barnum was right.

      A tie-dyed jock strap
      on the lower half of a broken equine manikin
      was a visual—almost spiritual statement
      on the evolution of man—a footnote on woman
      was a tampon, lit like a Fourth of July firework,
      aimed at the moon—a moon
      made of mold-encrusted cheese served
      with chilled dandelion wine—fermented,
      bottled and bonded in a micro-distillery,
      winery and brewery—in Brooklyn—known as
      Faux Bronx Cheers.

      A gorilla dressed as a man
      in a zebra-striped tuxedo greeted visitors
      to the gallery with the cranial skeletal remains
      of a porpoise or whale or whatever-it-was
      in his outstretched hand—contemplating.

      The rubble of the aftermath
      of a terrorist bomb would silt the gallery's display—
      providing puzzling, provocative
      and profound theories for anthropologists
      and archaeologists of the thirty-fifth century—
      weren't our fore bearers complex—
                         yet quaint?

Too many bubbles, too little wine, rank spores
on the cheese—the petrified, rancid cheese—
cats should pee in the litter
and man should not ...
        make bombs!
         8/01/07

What Have the Children Done?
inspired by *Echo of a Scream* [some forty years ago]

   The scale of good and evil
      cannot be balanced by a child.
      Nor has he or she the choice
      of parents, home or worldly things.

   Pregnant children of gas and gruel
      starving in bloating flesh,
      children suffering severed limbs,
      burns and death—
  What have they done ...
        What have the children done?

   Leaders claim to love children
      (of their own) but what of those of others
      Are they guilty by chance of birth—
      their poor choice of mothers?
  What have they done ...
        What have the children done?

   Their future stolen
      by the present and the past
      each child paying his debt in life—less living
      The future bounty of nature's wealth
      already spent with interest—
  What have they done ...
        What have the children done?

The child who grows to be
>> a soldier or a mother—
>> neither has a choice—their fate—
>> decided by another.
Dying in a far-off land in wars they never started
>> their children slain by guns, disease or lack of food ...
What have they done ...
>> >> What have the children done?

And then a child, a precocious child
>> strikes a note—a chord so strong and sweet
>> Or smiles with flashing eyes
>> when friends and family meet—
>> What evil stalks its young and loving prey—
>> Lurking there within us all?
What have they done ...
>> >> What *have* the children done?
>> >> >> 4/30/06

Her Eyes

Her eyes
>> lay pleading within red scars
> a mask,
>> not to hide, but
>> >> to shame those
>> >> >> who would do such things

The fires
>> still burn from the ruins
> the bomb,
>> fertilizer and oil
>> >> farming was good
>> >> >> the harvest bad!

The cowards
> brave, hidden away
>> no one,
>>> yet, had claimed responsibility
> they will
>> they always do

The bodies
> charred and ruined
innocents
> of a world gone mad
>> yes, someone is guilty
>>> but others guiltier

The stench
> a moistened cloth
>> does not contain the vile odor
burned flesh
> on the altar of sacrifice
>> by savage men
>>> to more savage gods

Those men
> freedom fighters? Soldiers?
what scars
> had they bourne
>> what losses suffered
>>> what hate within?
>>>> those men,
>>>>> the others

The wars
> go on forever
they have
> always,
>> back to the dawn of man
>>> why?

    Those pleading eyes
            see no more
      those eyes
            that never flashed with hate
                    had they seen joy?
    Her eyes—
           closed—
                  at peace—
                            she rests ...
                            4/9/05

White Flags and Dear Sweet Flowers
inspired by Jim Barry's field of flags Rt. #213 Chestertown, MD
and dedicated to those who paid the ultimate price.

The field of white flags, three thousand strong,
Cooled by breezes lamenting there in song
Began to overwhelm the space in the grass—
Young lives lost—too soon—much, much too fast.

The flags now gone into retreat
The dead who faced not sad defeat
But **honored** are our daughters and sons
Victims of power, greed, road-side bombs and guns.

Each day new flags in fertile fields have grown
A memorial to those whose stars had shown
Those who'd given their lives—their all
Joining heroes with names—
                    carved on a black stone wall.

Lest we forget the young who gave
(The young, the proud—the brave)
The ultimate sacrifice that one person can
And died for us in some foreign, hostile land

Remember well and know for sure
Man's greed and hate and lust for war
His never learning lessons that history has shown
Will forever harvest those dear young flowers—
                that should have lived and grown.
                                  4/22/07

When Did Birds Stop Being Our Friends?

When did birds stop being our friends
And drive-by shooters take aim on our schools
What evil is driving these horrible trends
Is the world adrift—a ship of fools?

Is greed so blinding that rich men can't see
What a world without birds would eventually be
And children that grow up in a world of fear
Lacking the values once held so dear?
What self-destructive force would lead men to kill
The youth of our species and destroy its will—
Our hope for the future, our last recourse—
For profit and gain with no remorse?

Listen to the raven and shaman of old
Learn from history and stories too often told
Look around and decide what it is worth
To sell our souls ... destroy the birds—
                      and our mother earth.
                                8/02/07

When Man Regains His Soul
(Inspired by Doug Cutter's piping in Fountain Park)

One lone piper stood
Piping in the fountain park
Piping only as he could
At the edge of dark.

Six years from that fatal day
When planes and building fell
And as the piper walked away
Our hearts and eyes began to swell.

For memories of a world in change
And those who've paid the ultimate price
If only we could rearrange
Remake the world, undo their sacrifice.

When will despots see their faults
And terrorists get their due
And rich men open up the vaults
And share the wealth owned by few.

When profit-seeking, selfish men
Learn which riches really make man whole
Maybe, just maybe—that is when
Man will regain his soul.

9/11/07

The Invisible Man

How long had he been there?
I really couldn't say
I passed by there almost each day
And hadn't noticed—
He just materialized—
But not an apparition—
He was there—flesh and bone

And he had been there
Perhaps days, maybe months
Perhaps a year.
In my mind's eye
I now remember seeing him
Smiling, waving
Sitting relaxed in his
Old beat-up recliner chair.

Now that I think of it
He waved to all who passed
The loading dock where he 'lived'
Somehow he had established
That concrete pad
As his patio and living room
I think he had an old mattress
Behind the Demsi-dumpster.

I had wondered why security
Hadn't had him removed—
Surely to allow him
Residence there was to invite
The worst of our fears—
The fear of the unknown men
Who might just join him
And settle there—
They never did.

He survived on handouts
Well not exactly handouts
He swept a floor here and there
He may have carried bags to cars
He may have helped unload trucks
How had he been
So invisible to me?

He drank coffee on his 'patio'
Each morning while reading day-old news
Or last month's magazines
Or maybe last year's—
I don't know—
In his absence
I left books for him to read—
(Most still on the top ten lists)

He didn't know me
I didn't know him
I'm not sure he even read the books
Although I often saw them recycled
At a nearly new store
I hope they filled two appetites.

I spent time wondering—
Who he was—
Where he was from—
What had he done—
How he was able to live?

I don't remember his last wave
Was it last week, last month
Or maybe last year?
He was simply there then gone—
Just as he had appeared.

And now, as I periodically do
I ask myself why—
Why hadn't I asked *him*?
Who he was—
Where he was from—
What had he done—
How he was able to live?

                          10/19/07

Right The Wrong

The morning sky burst forth in red
The clouds flowed in scarlet flame
Gentle breezes caressed the pond—
The shrubs and trees beyond.
Fall's brilliant colors muted at first dawn
Spring forth like fairies as they dance along—
The woodlands and the ridge
The ivy vines that form a twisting bridge
From nature's greatest beauty
To the poem hidden deep within.

Leaves from green to fall's bright colors burn
Setting a fire within the soul to yearn
And thus bursts forth in humblest imitation
This imperfect reflection of God's creation
The colors less than truly seen
The images, faulty as they are,
Are all that mortal man can glean
Would that he could shape a star.

Would that he could sing a song
Right the world and do no wrong
Write the stories in verse and rhymes
Of man's elevation to better times

Where love is pure and hatred dead
And man will cherish the rose instead
Of power, lust and greed
And with fervent passion—
                care for those in need.
                10/23/07

Section V. Spirituality:
Man's Never-ending Search for Meaning

The Light

The light
bright—
blue shimmering white
the beginning,
the all, the end.

Some say
that all life,
and all that is,
is purest energy.

A light form
from which all are born—
a red, red rose—
its prickly thorn.

A common will creates
the *us*, the *you*—the *me*.
A mountain
a river, a tree—
light is all you see.

A flower
blowing in a breeze
is what
the common host agrees.
Are atoms *thought*
in purest form?
Who creates
a raging storm?

The ebb and flow
of human time is
measured—
then it's done.
Light emits eternally—
and there
good and evil
merge as one.
                7/18/07

And All That Was, Was

In the void all was still
And all that was, *was*
And from that dark and empty space—
Light—a tiny spark of light—shown, *and was*
And soon the least became the great, *and was*.

Brilliance now shared the void
And cold encased the flame
The crystals grew with molten heat
And burst forth in chaos grand.

Shards of ice and light in space
Air and earth and clouds
Stars and planets filled the void
Light was shed and breezes blew.

And the earth shuddered in its wake
Mountains grew and land did quake
Clouds shed tears and winds embraced the sky
Rivers wound their winding way to flood the seas.

And mother earth's ripened womb
Spit forth life in many forms
Nature's children and Adam's sons
In gardens lived their lives as one.

And Eve one day an apple ate
At the bidding of a hissing snake
And from that time the earth was doomed
Man would dig his final tomb.

Man then invented gods
Until one and only one was said to be *the* One
Holy See and rites prevailed
And holy men became as God.

And all who worshiped Him
And Him alone, did say they knew *the* One
They fought and killed to prove them right
He of course looked on.

And as man grew intolerant
He slew his fellow man
He even killed the earth and air—
The seas and all within.

And then again the earth was bare
And space was just a void
Then darkness was all that was
And then a spark appeared ...
                              2/06/06

I Saw Within The Mountain

Although the path was old
It now was new to me
Every length and twisting turn—
I'd walked this path before.

I was a single, pilgrim traveler
But somehow not alone
I sensed a multitude
But them I could not see.

A great red oak stood in my path
One I'd never seen—
And yet I had—
Among the many trees.

Its brown and yellow leaves
The veins that formed a web
Every leaf itself was grand
Each leafy map—a story told.

The bark though rough
Had smoothness of its own
Traveled by legions of ants
Building tunnel homes.

The songs of birds though muted
Sang sweetly in my head
I arose into their flight
And soared above the trees.

The rivers and the valleys
Every hill and stream
While hidden in the fog
Were crystal clear to me.

I saw the shifting pebbles
Beneath a meadow stream
Eggs of frogs and fishes—
Polished diamonds in the sand.

I saw within the mountain
And all the passing stars
The journey swift—has taken many years
And yet an instant in my mind.

I once was the mountain—
The flowing meadow stream
And from the tree
Sprang forth my soul.

I look within and see not me
Not my earthly form
But all that flows within—
The all of everything.
                    2/20/06

The Voyeur

I guess I am a voyeur of sorts
Sitting, watching
Giving witness to all I see and hear
The sound of a mourning dove
Two strangers walking
Hand in hand
An expression of their love.

I ponder as I navigate
The many twists and turns of life
Who is that man down on the corner—
Homeless, seeking pocket change
Did he ever have a home—
A dog, children and
A loving wife?

I've seen majestic mountains
Heard the babble of trout streams
The whisper of a sweet soft breeze
As it meanders through
A stand of tall pine trees.

I remember December seven
nineteen forty-one
As a child of seven I could not fathom
What it meant for a nation
To engage in war—
Never thinking, never dreaming
That I would witness many more.

Cloistered in a town of white
I did not know the plight of blacks
And then a rifle sang out loud
A quiet hush among the crowd
A king was killed that fateful day
What price for freedom
Do some men have to pay?

I watched a young man age then die
My mother, too, joined him
On the journey mortals are forced to take
The pain and suffering along the way—
And to this day
I sit and wonder—Why?

I watch the TV talking heads
See children starving in far-off lands
Bombs exploding in market places
The horror expressed in strangers' faces
Hurricanes and tidal waves
Mountains spewing molten rock and smoke
Entire villages wiped from the face of earth
In a single stroke.

And as I sit and ponder
I realize that I am not alone
For somewhere way out beyond the stars
Sitting on His regal throne
Is the greatest voyeur of them all
The One who creates a mountain
Just to sit and watch it fall.
      10/14/07

The Voice

Who are you
Who speaks to me
In the voice of a mocking bird
The hiss of a coiled snake
And the whisper
of a soft sweet breeze?

Are you the memories
Of distant pasts
A collective wisdom
Hidden in the deep recesses
Of the minds of man—
Thoughts imbedded at conception?

Forgotten by a newborn babe
As innocence fades
And life invades—
Writing memories anew
For a future day

And as we grow
Lessons learned guide us
Along a path that we alone
Must choose

Through times of trial
Hurt and loss
A voice—unclear—whispers,
Urging us along the way

And if we but stop and listen
To our spirit guides
We may—just may—
Find the answer in that *one place*
                Where the voice resides.
                          9/25/07

Who Knows Where

Layers of clouds
        billowing white and gray
        in skies of blue
        birds in flight twist
        contrails of outbound planes
        off to who knows where—
                who knows where.

Clouds of dust
        shifting in the wind
        ghost crabs skitter
        over dunes of sand
        waves crash on shining shores
        seashells tumble with polished stones
        footprints seem to go on
        and on forever
        off to who knows where—
                who knows where.

Two lovers walking,
> laughing hand in hand
> a barking dog bites at waves
> while rushing out of reach
> does anyone ever notice
> others on the beach? The ebb
> and flow of daily tides
> a heat mirage that's there then gone
> off to who knows where—
>> who knows where.

Layers of clouds
> and shifting sand
> seas that roll and roar
> lovers walking, barking dogs
> shorebirds disappearing
> ghost crabs floating
> over grains of sand—and me—
> lost in thoughts of those I've loved
> and those who have gone on before
> off to who knows where—
>> who knows where ...
>> 9/20/07

Man's Merciful God

Bards have spoken of God and man
And a world created by Divine plan
Of goodness and mercy and servitude
What of this God to whom they allude?

What mercy is shown to a dying child
Caught up in war and a world gone wild?
Or a cancer patient gaunt and weak
Is this the mercy that Christians seek?

Ah yes, it's man's free will
The urge to rule and even kill
To bear one's pain and cruel assault
By faith to know it's not *God's* fault!

A forest fire consumes a deer, an elk—a bear
Is this the mercy that God's creations share?
Yet man prays to this kind God—
His discipline: spare not the rod.

Where was God when man arose
Saw the sun and smelled a rose
And conjured reason why
There was an earth and heaven's sky?

Were not the gods that man knew then
The gods who formed his life—his ken?
Were they not as kind *and cruel*
As the One who gave the Golden Rule?

What myth so powerful did evolve
That man would give his life—his last resolve
To some force unknown—the undefined
This absent God—benevolent and kind?

Blind is man who does not see
Through a life of toil and misery
That he alone can find his way
And live life well each new day.

The light within—that inner voice
The force that gives man *the* choice
His destiny is his alone
His and *only his* alone!
       2/02/06

The Time Has Come
(inspired by the BSO's rendition of Gustav Mahler's
Symphony No 2, 'Resurrection')

The time has come
The time *has* come
For all deceased to rise as one
The souls of all who've gone before
Arise and seek that foreign shore.

Life was given to live then die
A testing ground for wings to fly
To temper steel and grind down stone
No one can take this path alone.

Through sickness, health and happy times
Funeral dirges and wedding chimes
One walks this winding path called life
A balanced journey of joy and strife.

One must listen and be alert
To savor pleasure and endure the hurt
To live a life full and giving
A life of hope and love worth living.

The light that's seen at the very end
Illuminates the soul to comprehend
A whole new world never known
Now in purest light is shown.

The time has come
The time *has* come
For all deceased to rise as one
The souls of all who've gone before
Arise and seek that foreign shore.
                              6/12/06

The Soul

Some Native American Tribes
    believe that their spirits
    return to soar
    as eagles.
Others believe
    their souls
    return as butterflies.

The soul is the ether of life
    born from all that is known
    to reside in living things,
    to live to learn and return
    to infuse with a greater known.

As bear it learns the way
    of the woods, meadows,
    mountains and streams
As fish the ebb and flow
    of time and tides of the sea
As tiger the cunning
    and caring of cubs

As eagle the grace of the skies
    and nature's magnificent scenes
As monarchs the beauty of flowers,
        thistles and thorns
        and guidance for migrating souls

As man, a vessel to learn,
        to question to preserve
        or destroy.

The soul transcends
  all that is living
    all that has been
      and all that ever will be.
          12/07/06

Over Yonder
(Dedicated to John, Brenda and Kelly Foehrkolb)

Mommy, where is over yonder?
Why do you ask, my dear?
Uncle Herb told me that a cow—
                was over yonder.
I asked the farmer standing by the cow
where is over yonder?
He mused, "why, that house
                just beyond the bridge."

The house is our home so I asked Daddy
where is over yonder?
He thought and said, "over by that tree
                and behind the mountains"

So, Mommy, really,
where *is* over yonder?
"Well, dear, I guess you could say
that over yonder is over there
and back here again
                and just about everywhere."

Oh, Mommy, Mommy, thank you so very much
that makes it very clear
That *is* the answer
I have longed to hear
I asked preacher last Sunday
where God lives
And he said, "Kelly dear—
                God lives over yonder."

                            4/22/05

Part VI. Emotions and Feelings: Love and Relationship

Abstract Art

Her art,
abstract—
was strange to me
swirls of color
geometric design

an eye, an ear
disembodied—
floating in air
a cloud pedestal
rays of sun
on setting moon

blood drop tears
sands of sea, stone
and jellyfish
planets and microbes
two point perspective—
ten vanishing points

she takes me
to places unknown—
places
I know
I've been.
        12/09/06

Sometimes I Cry

I felt like crying—
I don't know—
It just welled up in me.

I saw a smiling,
beaming baby girl
hands, arms and legs
all dancing—as
babies are oft to do.

I heard a symphony
playing Ave Maria.
I saw a candle flicker
and then I thought of you.

A painted picture
called to me
from a darkened corner
of a gallery.

A young man sat
on legless stumps. He
raised his head and smiled at me,
"this was not within my plans—
I went to war
to keep our country free."

Sometimes mom or dad returns—
they've been gone away so long—
their graves half hidden in the grass
their memories come then gone so fast
Then I hear that special song—

I think of life and of death
and traveled roads I had taken
Of life's great pleasures
from majestic heights
to deepest depths—and
of one who came
and then *He* was forsaken.

A young child, a crippled bird
a mellow song, a picture
or a single word. Young men
lost to war not knowing
what life had in store ...

I sometimes cry
I don't know why
It just wells up in me ...   1/30/07

A Child, A Flower, A Poignant Memory

Smiling, she reached out
Her tiny right hand
In it was a small blue blossom
A single corn flower bloom—

Her matching eyes danced in cadence
With her twisting left hand
Her knees knocked together
As shyly she swayed in the breeze.

She looked at me—
A perfect stranger—
With pure innocence and trust
As she presented that treasure.

Then a glance to her mother
Who proudly nodded approval
The flower suspended mid-air.

As if in slow motion
Drawn by some conflicting magnetic force
I reached down to rescue the bloom
Those frozen seconds imprinted forever.

She squealed with glee
As I caught the flower
And fastened it to my jacket's lapel
I tipped my hat—she curtsied—
And sorry to say,
I never saw that sweet dear child again.
        10/10/07

I, The Man*

I
The man
Sitting next
To you right here
Have feelings to share
You, being unaware
Must think that I am foolish
My raw-nerve feelings just for you
Encourage a shy young man to speak
But the words in my mind I fear to say.
        10/15/07

*Written in Ertheree form

Life Without You
(Robert Burns's Birthday - 25 January 1759- 21 July 1796)

To compare your beauty to a rose
would fail to see the fire that burns within,
the warmth you share with me.
The rose's bloom comes but once a year,
yours will always flower in me
As night will surely follow day
My love will be with thee.

To compare you with the ocean deep
would overwhelm the sea
A vision short of the forest
for a single tree
The depth of my love for thee
is exceeded only by its breadth
Our love will survive this life
and live beyond our death.

To share our love and live as one
is as fresh each day as the rising sun.
If life was given for another purpose
I cannot see
        what life or living
                without you would be.
                              1/25/07

They Live In Memories
a poem inspired by
Bainbridge Elementary School's 4th Graders.

Everyone has felt sad
At one time or another.
The loss of a father
A mother
A sister, or a brother—
Brings dark clouds
Maybe even tears
They leave behind memories
Or sadly—
      your worst fears.

A dog that simply ran away
Or a cat
That up and died
One day
Or a dying doe on your back lawn
Giving birth
To a spotted fawn
Why, you wonder do they die
Why must I hurt so
And
Why do I have to cry?

When trees die in a forest
They give birth to the new
Life is a challenge
A constant test
To deal with grief
Makes a stronger—
Better you
To lose a loved one befalls us all
Everyone has to answer
When he hears the call.

How you treat these sad occasions
Life's harsh bumps
And cruel abrasions
Will decide how
You choose to grow.
You ask, "How do I,
The poet,
Know?"

You see my mom and dad
have not really gone away
They live within
And are with me
Every single day.
They are in my smile, the way I think
The very words I say.
Those I've known and loved
Have given strength to me
And forever they shall live—
                    Within my memory.
                        5/24/07

Hands

His huge hands
were calloused and scarred
shucking oysters and gutting fish
had taken its toll.
Ebony like fine grained wood
pink where knives had strayed
gouging sinew, skin and bone.
Waxen now—as he lay alone.

Her hands were porcelain smooth
snow white—delicate hands
steepled skyward
in solemn prayer.
Long, slender fingers
manicured nails.
Stark contrast ties
bound them together.
Black pearls of her rosary—
           glistened with her tears.
               3/11/06

By The Roadside Selling Her Wares

She sat by the roadside
      selling her wares
Her horseless cart
      a bursting bounty
      of fruit and bread—
      scarred wood sides,
      iron-rimmed wheels and
      a hanging, rusted scale.

She read while she waited
      shaded by a white lace parasol
      tied to a wood-framed webbed chair.
A mocking bird sang melodies
      immune to roadside noise and fumes.

Her handwritten signs invite you
      to buy, to stop and visit awhile—
      a misspelled word crossed out
      and written over again. In the field
      her horse grazed on clover,
      wild weeds and grass.

        I stopped to buy unneeded produce
        and bread. She shyly weighed
        and bagged the purchases I had made.
        Lost for just the right words
        I simply turned and looked away.
        Other than thank you, she too,
        had nothing to say—other than
        what both of our eyes had said.

As I sit paring and eating
        a lush ripe peach, I think
        of her soft pink skin. Her flowing
        blond hair and sky blue eyes—
        sitting in the shade
        of her white lace parasol,
        by the roadside selling her wares.
                        7/13/07

Christina*

She lived in my village, did Christina
A simple girl, the joy of my life
Cunning and agile as her Persian cat
She had a passion for wine and flowers
Full of life her thoughts were of death
Her eyes, to her soul, a window.

I first saw her there in her bedroom window
And felt the sorrow of a mourning Christina
It was the day of her father's death
The start of my being, my life
I secretly sent her dozens of flowers
And took to tending Balou—her cat.

Ah yes, Balou the cat
He now sits and shares *my* bedroom window
Just sitting silently gazing at flowers
I sometimes mistakenly call him Christina
We had shared such a wonderful life
The young never think of death.

But on that day of her father's death
She felt not for me, herself nor her cat
She dwelled on her father's life
She wrote his name in the fog on the window
And sobbed and sobbed did sad Christina
She wept and cradled the proffered flowers.

Each day I sent a bouquet of flowers
I vowed to love her until our death
Such was my love for Christina
Our banns were witnessed by Balou the cat
Purring there in the small chapel window
Christina gave passion and purpose to life.

Together we lived and learned about life
We tended our garden—our many flowers
We'd sit each day and look out the window
Never thinking of death
We'd lived the nine lives of Balou the cat
I was taught to live and love by Christina.

Now I mourn each day for Christina
(I share my grief with Balou the Cat)
And await the day that I join her in death.
                                    8/18/07

* This is my first attempt at the Sestina form of poetry. A thirty-nine line poem of six stanzas, six lines each, ending with a seventh stanza, the envoi (envoy), of three lines. Each line ends with one of six words in a specific order. The envoi lines end in three of the words i.e 1,3,5; 2,4,6 etc.

He Heard The Bells

As he awoke he heard the bells
Strange,
He had never heard the bells before.

The sun was hidden by the clouds
The traffic
Made not a roar or single sound.

The birds sat muted in the trees
Not a chirp
Not one trilling song.

The snow was cold and deep
The pond
A frozen sheet of ice.

The children skated silently
The crack
Opened quickly, quite deadly.

In seconds they were gone
Mittens and a cap
Remained upon a skim of ice.

He dove into the chilling pond
Grasped
Their tiny, soft-cold hands.

The frigid water became a friend
They drifted
In a silent, frozen dream.

As he awoke
And saw a light
He heard the soundless bells ...
                                  2/16/06

She Blushes

Beautiful—is not the first word to mind
but beautiful she is
mellow Mediterranean-toned skin
a reserved gentle smile
eyes doing her laughing for her

Shy—when complimented she blushes
moving to less personal things
she moves on taking others' orders
as her sweet presence drifts away

Her hair gives ebony frame
to a perfect oval of face
her eyes ever so slightly smile
pupils hidden in dark liquid brown
intelligence and breeding present
a glint—hints of naughtiness—
an unknowing teasing charm

Her cheeks high
falling gently to perfect lips
that subtly shift with each new emotion

Neck and shoulders
crafted like smooth sculptured marble
breasts gently imprint
her black chiffon sheath dress
smooth sensual conflicting curves
of waist and hips
A slightly raised triangular mound
begins the long languid
flow of her legs
to feet—tiny and perfectly formed

No, beautiful does not jump to mind—
she is exquisite!

4/4/04

Section VII. For Fun:
   Into Every Life There Should Be Injected Fun

Just About Everything
Inspired by the Bainbridge Elementary 4th graders

What is it about a sunrise or sunset
Or the way the moon glows—
The silence when it snows
The feeling that you get—

When stars shine bright at night
A silhouetted deer just there out of sight
Dancing rain on new made lakes
The smell of mother's baking cakes—

The cooing of a mourning dove
The heartbreak of a teenage love
A young girl's soothing lullaby
Calming babies when they cry—

The babble of a cool trout stream
Glistening pebbles that glint and gleam
Snow-capped mountains reaching high
Seeking purchase in Montana's sky—

The endless waves that pound the shores
Then shush away from grand loud roars
A crying gull from far off somewhere
The smell of fresh salt ocean air—

The sound of fall's first honking geese
The loving smile of a nephew or a niece
A teacher's timely "well done" cheer
When something hard becomes so clear—

What is it that makes us cry or laugh
A tumbling clown, a dancing bear, a circus tall giraffe?
What is it that makes us write or sing?
I'd say just about everything—
Yes ...   just about everything ...
\hfill 5/15/07

A Little Bit of This And ...

In everyone's life there is
a little bit of this and
a lot of that and
all that ties the two. Memories
of a childhood prank—those
we've lost, forgot to thank.
A heron barking in the wind
above the setting sun. A soul
set free to roam.
Another life begun.

Sitting in the coffee shop
chatting up some friends—
local news, political views
and the market trends. The
music of chatter as dishes clatter—
what does it matter, it's
just another day. That
may be so—yes,
that may be so—but
should I work or play?

Each day starts again anew
the grass is wet from morning dew—
sunrise yet another hew—
so little time so much to do. Shall
I paint the shed today or
take my leave and run away. Will
the lottery favor me
pay my bills and set me free?

Life is just a smorgasbord
no morsel there to be ignored
each lesson learned should lead toward
a greater life—a just reward. So I'll
try a little bit of this and a lot of that
and limit my excuses—and
love my dammed old shabby cat
and suffer its abuses.
                    7/17/07

Tithing The Cat

I tithe the cat—
unknowingly give him his share
from the food that I eat
to his perch in my favorite blue chair.

One tenth of my bacon
each morning he gets
and I, the moron,
the one who forgets—
who is the master
and who the pet.

Reclined in my chair
I relax and read
he stands at the door
as if in need—
I rush to the door
to let the cat out
he jumps in my chair—
it's his—no doubt!

Curled in a ball
he looks up at me,
"it *is* my chair,
don't you see?"

At night while I'm lying
comfortably in my bed
he roams outside searching
for something in the shed—
At 4:00 a.m.
it's time to come in—
is tithing a cat
a mortal sin?

He's fed gourmet meals
every single day
he hoards his food
in a sly cat's way.

Then out the door he goes
begging for food
from sympathetic neighbors he knows
("Poor cat—he's misunderstood.")

He comes and goes
as he darn well pleases
every advantage
he quickly seizes.

Love from a cat
is a very strange thing
he'll rub off his hair
on what your wearing
(he'll roll on his back
on anything black!)

He'll ignore you for hours
and hours on end
and just when you're busy
a clear message he'll send—
he'll jump in the middle
of your project at hand
get your attention—
defiant and daring he'll stand.

As quickly he came
he's gone in a flash—
he's taken his aim
and then a loud crash—
he pounces on an imagined mouse
that he proudly carries around the house.

He walks with stealth on chairs
and around picture frames
putting on airs
as your cheese snack—he claims—

And just when you've had
enough of that cat
he'll bring you a present
and remind you that—
he loves you in that cat strange way
he spends his nine lives trying to say
it is for him that you were put here
and to tithe the cat—isn't it clear?

          12/11/06

Roaches Rule

I saw a cockroach write
in white flour on the floor
around midnight ...

He wrote in a cockroach-like scrawl
His words meandered wherever he'd crawl
He wrote of things unknown to man
Of times about when the world began
For cockroaches were here long before us
And being that old gives him an edge—a plus.

He comes out at night when he can't be seen
He hides in places where mothers can't clean
If one can be seen you can be sure
There are hundreds in the walls and under the floor
When you don't see them and think they're all gone
One jumps up to greet you as you mow the lawn.

Some say that roaches can talk
I've never heard a word, a scream or a squawk
But I have read a story written by one
Of cockroach humor and sense of fun.

Like mice they like to sneak around
Performing their tricks and acting like clowns
I've even seen one roll over, play dead like an opossum
But in a blink of an eye he's gone instead—how
                awesome!

They used to crawl on cavemen's floors
They somehow arrived on all of earth's shores
Roaches are everywhere and yet they are not
For years they'll just hide—to plan and plot.

When dinosaurs died and most species too
Populations of roaches just grew and grew
And when all humans have passed away
The roaches will rule, frolic and play.
                              4/22/07

Do Goldfish Have a Soul?

I had a goldfish that one day died
I sat and worried, shook and cried
It had been my golden friend
Right up to the bitter end.

I'd watch him swim and splash with glee
The silent words he spoke to me
Through bubbles in his grand round bowl—
Do goldfish have a soul?

There was a treasure chest in which he hid
Forced air would open and close the lid
He'd dart in and out of that box
Sly was he as a gray-red fox.

The day I found out that he was a she
Was when she laid a thousand eggs for me
And when they hatched they were a plenty
My fish bowl couldn't hold that many.

So I gathered all of Mom's deep dishes
Against her kind, firm mother wishes
And divided all the eggs just so
Then watched them squiggle, swim and grow.

So large did all the fish become
I gave almost all away—but some
I still have swimming in a large fish bowl
And yes—I do think goldfish have a soul.
                                    5/28/07

Crickets, Black Roosters and Crows

The crickets are playing their hind leg fiddles
they play for their supper reciting their riddles
First far off and then so near
They always return in the fall of the year.

A chirp from a hide in the living room where
I search in the fireplace, my favorite chair
Under the sofa and everywhere
He plays unimpeded without a care.

Like a ventriloquist he throws his voice
Hidden away in a place of his choice
At night when I am almost asleep
I hear a sound—a cheep, cheep, cheep.

With flashlight in hand I jump out of bed
While I should be sleeping I'm hunting instead
For that black intruder invading my night
Stealthily creeping there just out of sight

At last I have him caught in the corner
Sitting there like Little Jack Horner
He leaps for freedom just out of my reach
And returns to singing his high-pitched screech.

Hidden away, his silence a rouse
Knowing the hunt I cannot refuse
We play at his game 'til just about dawn
I find him and catch him and then he's gone.

I crawl into bed as he silently sleeps
But into my dreams his memory creeps
And into a nightmare it grows and grows
A chorus of crickets, black roosters and crows.
                                    11/08/06

Ants Work—Cats Play

An industrious ant
crosses a stone in the yard.
The cat goes crazy—
those darting paw jabs—a hiss,
          and a hop in the air.

The ant unaware
attacks a fallen leaf.
The cat circles its prey—
it dances sideways—retreats,
          lays low in the grass.

The ant twitches its antennae
cuts the leaf to manageable size
and carries her burden on.
The cat is in hot pursuit—
of dandelion down and
          bird chirps from the trees.
                  12/1/06

Hash House Harriers

The Hash House Harriers of Kuala Lumpur
Have run millions of miles—maybe ten more
Back in nineteen hundred and thirty eight
Sitting in a hash house they drank and ate
(They did not smoke weed or local hash
They preferred beer—paying in cash!)

English officers—gentlemen they were
Before drink—exercise, they did prefer
Through tropical jungle they laid out a course
Exercise and conscience—their driving force
Dressed in khaki they would run for miles
Natives watched with great confused smiles.

They ran through swamp and scraggly bush
Ever farther and onward they'd proudly push
Through those jungles of Kuala Lumpur
Leaving them tired and so very soar
Back to the hash house the harriers would run
There to drink beer and have serious fun.

The tradition has carried on through the years
The harriers run on encouraged by cheers
For exercise and good causes they still run
Few are left from the tradition begun
By English officers in days of yore
In that wee hash house in Kuala Lumpur!

4/5/04

The Leaf

The leaf, veined and withered,
Fluttered slowly to the earth
Soon to be ground to dust
By passing cars and wind—
Never knowing its origins
Its purpose or design
It had never met its roots
Nor seen within the rings—
Soon to be one with the soil
Ingested by the tree
Making it whole again.

12/01/07

About the Author

The author: ENNWR
Photograph by John Foehrkolb

Howard McIntyre is a former principal in Kent County, Maryland. He began his career in Baltimore County as a teacher of mathematics and science and retired in 1993 as the Director of Staff Development for the Calvert County Public Schools. McIntyre began his retirement years as an education consultant. Two years later he was sure that he had made the right decision about retirement. Kayaking, birding, photography and volunteer work became his passion. He has logged over 4,000 volunteer hours at Eastern Neck and Black Water National Wildlife Refuges and additional hours as a board of directors member for the Kent County Adult Medical Day Care Center.

McIntyre has paddled most of the rivers, ponds and bays of the Eastern Shore of Maryland. He has birded many areas of the Delmarva Peninsula, Ohio River Valley, Pacific Northwest, New England and Nova Scotia. His photography was featured in an exhibit in Chestertown, Maryland, in 2007. His photography and poetry are displayed and sold at the Rock Hall Gallery in Rock Hall, Maryland.

After taking The Pleasure of Poetry course offered in the Life Long Learning Program at Washington College in Chestertown, Howard's creative juices were flowing. Since this awakening in 2004 he has written over 400 poems. McIntyre has shared his poetry via readings at the Prince Theatre, Play it Again Sam, Andy's in Chestertown and The Mainstay in Rock Hall, Maryland. He has also worked with students through the Poet in Residency Program. The themes of Howard's poetry and photography vary widely.